Alaskan Forget Me Nots

Sarah Jack

Order this book online at www.trafford.com
or email orders@trafford.com

Most Trafford titles are also available at major online book retailers.

Print information available on the last page.

ISBN: 978-1-4669-8945-0 (sc)
ISBN: 978-1-4669-8944-3 (e)

Trafford rev. 05/05/2017

 www.trafford.com

North America & international
toll-free: 1 888 232 4444 (USA & Canada)
phone: 250 383 6864 ♦ fax: 812 355 4082

1

have keep us
direct to love life gives.
Lord Jesus Christ!

6

13

21

Rejoice in the Lord Jesus Christ!

24

25

30

40

41

Praise the
Lord Jesus Christ!

love you,
Lord Jesus Christ,

Rejoice!

Joy!

Thank you Lord
Jesus Christ!

I love you!

Grace +
faith in the
Lord Jesus
Christ!
amen

Thank-you
Lord for
are
food!

Lord do you still love me I still love you and need you!

Sweet Leah

81

111

114

Printed in the United States
By Bookmasters